ANIMALS Are NOT Like US

DOGS

For a free color catalog describing Gareth Stevens Publishing's list
of high-quality books and multimedia programs, call 1-800-542-2595
(USA) or 1-800-461-9120 (Canada). Gareth Stevens Publishing's Fax:
(414) 225-0377. See our catalog, too, on the World Wide Web: gsinc.com

Library of Congress Cataloging-in-Publication Data

Meadows, Graham.
    Dogs / by Graham Meadows.
      p. cm. — (Animals are not like us)
    Includes bibliographical references and index.
    Summary: Describes the physical characteristics and behavior
of dogs, pointing out ways in which they differ from people.
    ISBN 0-8368-2252-8 (lib. bdg.)
    1. Dogs—Juvenile literature. 2. Dogs—Physiology—Juvenile
literature. [1. Dogs.] I. Title. II. Series: Meadows, Graham.
Animals are not like us.
SF426.5.M435   1998
636.7—dc21   98-18763

North American edition first published in 1998 by
Gareth Stevens Publishing
1555 North RiverCenter Drive, Suite 201
Milwaukee, WI 53212 USA

Original edition published in 1998 by Scholastic New Zealand Limited,
21, Lady Ruby Drive, East Tamaki, New Zealand. Original © 1998 by
Graham Meadows. End matter © 1998 by Gareth Stevens, Inc.

Printed in the United States of America

1 2 3 4 5 6 7 8 9 02 01 00 99 98

ANIMALS Are NOT Like US
DOGS

Graham Meadows

Gareth Stevens Publishing
MILWAUKEE

Dogs are not like us.

Dogs don't see colors like we do.

The world looks black, white,
and gray to a dog.

Most dogs'
eyes are
brown.

A few have
gray eyes.

Dogs are not like us.

Dogs can hear sounds much better than we can.

They can even hear a special dog whistle, which is too high-pitched for our ears.

Dogs' ears are a different shape from ours.

Some are floppy.

Some are pointed.

Some you can't see at all.

Dogs are not like us.

They can smell scents that we can't.

They spend a lot
of time sniffing
around things.

The scents they smell tell them
a lot about their world.

They can tell what other animals have
been there, and how long ago.

Dogs are not like us.

Their tongues are different from ours.
Dogs have long, wet, pink tongues.

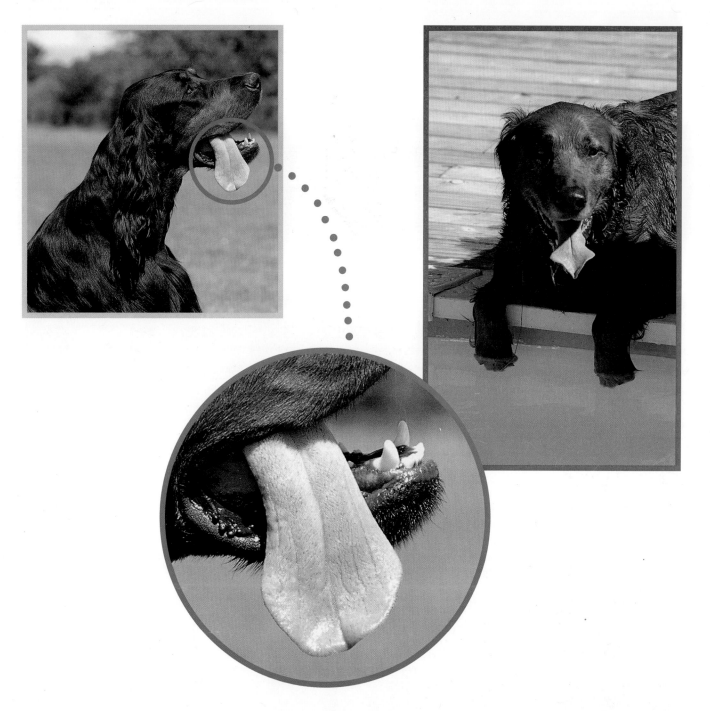

When dogs are hot, they pant with their tongues out.

This helps cool them down.

Dogs are not like us.

They stand and walk on four legs, so most of them can run faster than us.

Dogs' feet, or paws, are not like ours.

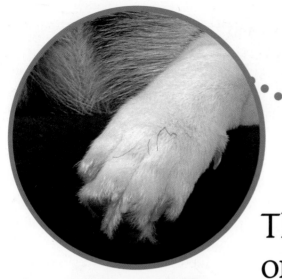

They have five pads on each foot, which act as cushions.

Their toenails are called claws, and they are long and pointed.

Sometimes they need trimming.

Dogs are not like us.

Dogs talk to each other in different ways. They whine, bark, growl, and howl.

When a dog is scared, it puts its tail between its legs.

Dogs also use their tails to show how they feel. They all wag their tails when they're happy.

Dogs' tails come in all shapes and sizes.

But there is one way in which dogs are like us.

They like eating!

Glossary

· ·

bark *(v)* — to make a noise similar to a short, loud cry. *When an animal, such as a dog, **barks**, it is a way for it to communicate its feelings in a particular situation.*

claws — the sharp and sometimes curved nails on the toes of dogs and other animals. *Dogs have **claws** that are long and pointed.*

cushion *(n)* — an object that is similar to a pad or a pillow that softens a hit or step. *Dogs have pads on the bottom of their feet that act as **cushions** when they walk or run.*

different — not the same. *There are many **different** shapes and sizes of dogs' ears, as well as many **different** kinds of dogs.*

floppy — not stiff; able to droop. *Some kinds of dogs,* like the cocker spaniel, have very **floppy** ears.

growl — the low, deep, rumbling sound made by some animals, such as dogs, when they are afraid or when danger is nearby. *A dog might **growl** if it is approached by a stranger or another dog.*

high-pitched — having a very high sound, such as that of some whistles. *Dogs can hear a special kind of dog whistle, which is too **high-pitched** for our ears.*

howl — a long, wailing cry, like the sound made by a dog, wolf, or coyote. *A dog might **howl** if it wants to come into the house.*

pads — the cushions on the bottom of a dog's foot that help it walk or run. *Dogs have five **pads** on each foot.*

pant *(v)* — to take short, quick breaths. *Dogs **pant** with their tongues out to cool off when it is hot or when they are running or playing.*

pointed — coming to or having a sharpened end. *Some dogs' ears are **pointed**, and they may stand straight up.*

scared — afraid of something; frightened. *A dog might put its tail between its legs when it is **scared**.*

scents — the smells that come from various objects. *Dogs can tell if other animals have been in the area by sniffing for the **scents** the other animals left behind.*

shape — the outer form of an object; an outline. *Dogs' ears have different **shapes**, with some short and pointy and others long and rounded.*

sniffing — breathing in by taking short breaths through the nose.

*Some animals, such as dogs, smell objects by **sniffing**.*

toenails — the nails on the toes of a person or animal. *A dog's **toenails** are called claws, and they are long and pointed.*

trimming — cutting or clipping to make something shorter or even. *Long toenails on a dog curve under and need **trimming** or they will cause problems for the dog when it walks or runs.*

whine — to make a high, shrill sound or cry. *Dogs communicate in many different ways, sometimes with a **whine**.*

whistle *(n)* — an object that makes a high, clear sound when air is blown through it. *Dogs will usually come to their owners when they hear the sound of a special dog **whistle**.*

Activities

Make a Puppy Puppet

Make a cute puppy puppet with an old sock. Would you like it to have long ears or short ears, brown eyes or gray; will it be spotted or all one color? Use white glue to attach felt scraps, yarn, buttons, or other materials to make your puppy's eyes, mouth, and markings just the way you want them. Bunch up part of the sock with rubber bands to make your puppy's ears or nose. If you want, add other details, such as whiskers, with a felt-tip marker. Then slip your puppy puppet over your hand, and you're ready for a puppet show!

Ears to You!

Dogs' ears come in many different shapes and sizes, including some that are floppy and others that are pointed. Make a list of different kinds of animals that have ears that are floppy (like an elephant) or that are pointed (like a cat). Can you think of any other animals, besides dogs, that might belong on both lists?

Dog Show

Find a book that pictures different breeds of dogs. What is the biggest breed? The smallest? What was each breed's original purpose? Do the breeds still do this work?

How Nosy Are You?

Dogs can detect scents that humans cannot. Test your nose power by making mystery scent bottles. In small bottles, place various items, such as lemon juice, cinnamon, mint, banana, and so on. See if your friends and family members can identify each scent.

Books

Becoming Your Dog's Best Friend. Bill Gutman (Millbrook Press)

Dog. Juliet Clutton-Brock (Knopf)

Dogs. Gail Gibbons (Holiday House)

Dogs, Wild and Domestic. Markus Kappeler (Gareth Stevens)

A Dozen Dirty Dogs. William H. Hooks (Gareth Stevens)

It Could Still Be a Dog. Allan Fowler (Childrens)

Jack the Puppy. Jane Burton (Gareth Stevens)

Pete the Puppy. Gisela Buck and Siegfried Buck (Gareth Stevens)

Videos

Dog Care. (Home Line Video)

The Dog Family. (International Film Bureau)

Dogs. (Churchill Media)

Dogs, Cats and Rabbits. (Public Media, Inc.)

Friend for Life. (Pyramid Film & Video)

Pets: A First Film. (Phoenix/BFA)

Pets and Their Care. (AIMS Media)

Puppy Pals. (NorthStar Entertainment)

Web Sites

www.canismajor.com/dog/
  guide.html

homepages.ihug.co.nz/~
  meadows/animal.htm

www.akc.org/

www.bestfriends.org

Some web sites stay current longer than others. For further web sites, use your search engines to locate the following topics: *animals, dog breeds, dogs, humane society,* and *pets.*

Index

barking 16

claws 15
colors 6
cushions 15

ears 9
eating 18
eyes 7

feet 15

growling 16

hearing 8, 9
howling 16

legs 14, 16

pads 15
panting 13

scents 10, 11
seeing 6
smelling 10, 11
sounds 8

tail 16, 17
toenails 15
tongues 12, 13
trimming 15

wagging 17
whining 16
whistle 9

Former veterinarian Graham Meadows is the author and/or photographer of over seventy books for children about animals.

It was while working as a vet at the Aukland Zoo in New Zealand that Graham Meadows's interest in animal photography began. He finds the way animals look and behave endlessly fascinating. His desire to pass on this enthusiasm to a younger generation has led him to produce the *Animals are not like us* series for three- to seven-year-olds.